Break the silence, tell your truth.

LANCASHIRE

Edited By Wendy Laws

First published in Great Britain in 2019 by:

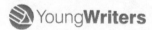

Young Writers
Remus House
Coltsfoot Drive
Peterborough
PE2 9BF
Telephone: 01733 890066
Website: www.youngwriters.co.uk

All Rights Reserved
Book Design by Spencer Hart
© Copyright Contributors 2019
Softback ISBN 978-1-83928-003-0
Hardback ISBN 978-1-83928-004-7
Printed and bound in the UK by BookPrintingUK
Website: www.bookprintinguk.com
YB0419X

FOREWORD

Since 1991 our aim here at Young Writers has been to encourage creativity in children and young adults and to inspire a love of the written word. Each competition is tailored to the relevant age group, hopefully giving each student the inspiration and incentive to create their own piece of creative writing, whether it's a poem or a short story. We truly believe that seeing their work in print gives students a sense of achievement and pride.

For our latest competition *Poetry Escape*, we challenged secondary school students to free their creativity and break through the barriers to express their true thoughts, using poetic techniques as their tools of escape. They had several options to choose from offering either a specific theme or a writing constraint. Alternatively they could forge their own path, because there's no such thing as a dead end where imagination is concerned.

The result is an inspiring anthology full of ideas, hopes, fears and imagination, proving that creativity really does offer escape, in whatever form you need it.

We encourage young writers to express themselves and address topics that matter to them, which sometimes means exploring sensitive or difficult topics. If you have been affected by any issues raised in this book, details on where to find help can be found at: **www.youngwriters.co.uk/support**.

CONTENTS

Broughton Business & Enterprise College, Broughton

Aamirah Khawaja (13)	1
Nicole Rosa Cornall (15)	2
Emma Burgess (14)	4
Ewan McLean (13)	6
Viki Clarke (13)	8
Mckenzie Baker (13)	10
Katie G E Wilkinson (14)	12
Indiana Moore (13)	14
Rabiyah Jamil (12)	16
Casey Olive (13)	18
Anna Smyth (13)	19
Megan Sloan (13)	20
Blake George Harrison (13)	22
Alisha Dahya (13)	23
Safa Beg (13)	24
Eleanor McWilliams (13)	25
Bobby Higham (13)	26
Noah Campbell Beith (13)	27
Lottie Carter (13)	28
Beth Barker (13)	29
Frances Grace Park (13)	30
Rory Hastings (13)	31
Amy Askam (13)	32
Libby Gibson (13)	33
Jenna Cross (13)	34
Hayden Cooke (13)	35
Emma Reynolds (13)	36
Rebecca Wright (13)	37
Aaisha Patel (13)	38
Harry Harmer (13)	39
Isaac Jones (13)	40
Emily Saunders (14)	41
Saira Latif (12)	42
Archie Macleod (13)	43
Rian Bowes (14)	44
Khadijah Patel (13)	45

Oulder Hill Community School, Rochdale

Heidi Elizabeth Walkden (13)	46
Naomi Borg (12)	48
Matilda Glendinning (12)	49
Aziz Ahmad	50
Laibah Sohail (12)	51
Igor Kadima	52
Rebecca Andrew & Libby Mort (12)	53
Zara Shaukat (13)	54
Aimee Louise Marland	55
Joel David Crabtree (12)	56
Aneesa Mahroof (12)	57

St Bede's High School, Blackburn

Liliana L Moore (12)	58
Enrikas Juselis (12)	60

St Gabriel's RC High School, Bury

Roan Schofield (13)	62
Maimoona Latif (13)	64

St Peter's RC High School, Manchester

Isaora Tandy Shima (12)	65
Glory Odubanjo	66
Alexa Murkste	68
Kieran Asif	70

Alicja Baczkowicz (13)	72
Arianna Voniece Arielle Allen (13)	73
Blake Joyce	74
Jennifer Adesanya (13)	75
Jessica Belle Stockley (13)	76
Khadija Irfan (13)	78
David Abioye (12)	79
Osasumwen Aimuyo (12)	80
Rianna Holden (12)	81
Keziah Kazadi (13)	82
Yahya Hussein (11)	83
Thandi Sibanda	84
Aliyah Soyinka (13)	85
Alisha Akram (12)	86
Nur-Aein Saidil (12)	87
Emma Louise Hennessy (14)	88
Modupe Olowu (13)	89
Gloria Kayenge (11)	90
Neo Cassidy (13)	91
Danny Bradley (12)	92
Jane Rosana (12)	93
Izodosa Divina Osarenmwinda (13)	94
Ashiq Ali Mirza (11)	95
Wiktoria Januszewska (13)	96
Melissa Nguyen-Le (13)	97
Joshua Lo (12)	98
Flourish Ugiagbe	99
Cheloliseh Joseph Umeh (12)	100
Roda Afeworki (13)	101
Dominion Ugiagbe (12)	102
Gamiel Bughaili (12)	103
Jakai Ucal McGlacken-Bryan (11)	104
Shadeh Stone	105
Fabian Truszkowski (12)	106
Angel Taofeeqah Jimoh (13)	107
Beauty Somoye (11)	108
Daniel Yemane Fesseha	109
Dipto Obyadur (12)	110
Kai Douglas (12)	111
Fatou Mbye (13)	112
Hamza Waseem (13)	113
Chanel Nicole May (12)	114
Divine Omose Omoijade (12)	115
Aaron Tebu (12)	116
Josephine Ashiru (13)	117

Walton-le-Dale High School, Bamber Bridge

Jessica Waite (13)	118

Home At Last

When I was a kid
I was the happiest girl I knew.
I had good friends,
A good family
And a good life.
All of that changed.
It all got torn away from me like Velcro.
We moved. And again. And again.
They were arguing about pathetic things
Whenever he came to see us.
I felt alone.
Nights were filled with tears that could fill an ocean.
Then we moved.
My first thoughts were anger.
But then she told me where, I was ecstatic.
We were going home. Back to him.
Finally,
Home at last
As a family.

Aamirah Khawaja (13)
Broughton Business & Enterprise College, Broughton

Fireflies

One autumn evening as summer came to a close
I sat underneath the honeysuckle tree
Its essence still smelt ripe and crisp - however, it was dying
Gone were the good ol' days when Papa came home
Now winter was on its approach.

The gruesome, spine-chilling and cunning winter
It covered the ground well, like my secrets
The long summer days were bleeding into nightfall
When God finally decides that his people
Do not need the company of daylight
He diminishes the light just like that.

Soft and disturbing new flakes caressed my skin
It felt like a cold, sharp tingle
I was prepared for the worst of it to come
I often turned to the fireflies as if they were an old friend
However, they too were slowly dying.

Sometimes I would see how many I could count
Before they were consumed by the greedy hands of darkness
Their bulbs flickered like old gas lamps
They had seen better days.

For God Himself could only tell me to leave
Leave this winter, wild wasteland

With tears prickling in my eyes, I gazed at the stars
Mesmerised by their glittering, dark dance

But who knows how long they would have
Before Jack Frost comes
Tearing and shredding lives away
Manipulating and confiscating joy.

Upon the crest of the mountain, some daylight remained
However, it too was dying
By the time I turned around, winter would be here
And as I did, the fireflies vanished
As if with discretionary power
Someone had switched them off.

I wept for the long days of summer
But I knew that the dark age would seem like an eternity.

Nicole Rosa Cornall (15)
Broughton Business & Enterprise College, Broughton

Anxiety And Depression

People think life is all fun and games,
Until you have anxiety and depression, then it all depends.
Sometimes they get bullied, sometimes it's at home
And most of the time
Others don't even know what's going on.
Anxiety and depression levels are rising...
Isn't that amazing?
Teenagers nowadays have the same level of anxiety
As people in the 1950s who were in mental asylums,
That's a fact!
And we are to blame.
They sometimes feel like they can't speak out about it
Because they're ashamed,
So every day, from when they wake up
To when they fall asleep,
They have a fake, gleaming smile
That rises up to their cheeks.
They hide their arms, they don't like their thighs
And how do I know this? Because it's all happened in my life.
It's a mental struggle to think everything's fine,
When in reality, you just really badly want to hide.
We need to raise awareness for all these people just like me
Who hate their weight, hair, eye colour,
Height, voice, face and even knees.
It's not funny what this generation has grown up to be,
Even if you may find it hard to believe.

Don't just ask somebody if they are okay
And walk away.
No, that's not how you help them out.
Just say, "Hi, I'm here for you. Don't worry.
If you ever need anything call me."
Because that's how they get it off their chest.
That's how you help, not just them, but other people too.
Then you help this generation turn into
Something better and new.

Emma Burgess (14)
Broughton Business & Enterprise College, Broughton

Changes

The world has changed,
people lie,
tell you your thoughts should be rearranged.

Evil people, telling you your mind is deranged,
but you're in your own cage,
feeling like you're slowly getting more insane.

People grow up believing things,
malicious minds twisting it like they are kings,
when you tell somebody, the bully just won't admit.

Extreme amounts of effort are wasted,
by self-conscious people trying to be perfect.

Perfect people don't exist, so why pretend to be one?
Don't change what you believe,
just by being told you're 'wrong'.

The young being influenced,
being told what to do and how to live,
by people who want to use them.

And set their confidence
and happiness on fire
in a blaze of corrupted words.

These flames are started by sparks
and sparks by people.

No one speaks their mind, they type it
and make the world define
itself by comment sections.

Why take advice
and complaints from people
who won't listen to yours?

It's like giving money
to someone pretending to be poor,
find some real friends,
they'll open multiple doors.

Just be the 'real you',
not the person when everybody is watching,
express your views
and open up your mind to new opportunities.

Ewan McLean (13)
Broughton Business & Enterprise College, Broughton

Sticks And Stones

'They may break our bones
But words will never hurt me'.
It's not true really, is it?
Words do hurt.
They really hurt!

Words are our strongest power,
They are our bullets,
They are our arrows
And words always hit their targets.

They always get their message across,
They always do their job,
They always satisfy their customer,
Words are stronger than sticks and stones!

Some people have shields,
But they are weak in the face of words.
Shields can't hide you forever,
Words break the toughest walls.

Stares in the corridors,
Whispers looming in the shadows,
Giggles as you pass,
Pointing fingers.

The judgement may not break your bones
But it hurts like it.

It breaks your spirit,
It takes the hope in your soul.

Words do hurt
More than broken bones.

But broken bones can be fixed
But hope is in short supply.
Spirit is hard to find,
Broken souls can't be mended.

Words leave the deepest scars,
Use your words wisely.

Viki Clarke (13)
Broughton Business & Enterprise College, Broughton

Flat Earth

I grew up believing that the Earth was flat,
That cucumbers were worms
And that life had no twists or turns.
I was wrong.
So wrong.
I can still remember the day I got my first nickname,
Flatty.
"Hey look, it's Flatty,
Speccy four eyes,
Dumb idiot,
Hobo,
Go die in a fire."
People didn't understand what depression was,
It wasn't a joke,
It wasn't made up,
It wasn't a disease,
People didn't understand anxiety,
Not wanting to go to school
Because you know that you will get laughed at,
Discriminated.
Ignored.
"You can't play with us, Flat Boy."
Anxiety isn't something that can be ignored,
It's always there
Eating into your thoughts,
Turning your life into a dark and twisted ghost train.

It doesn't care about you,
It doesn't give two hoots
And it will build up inside of you,
Feeding on your mind,
Well, Anxiety,
Tell the Devil I said hey,
You aren't going to affect me today.

Mckenzie Baker (13)
Broughton Business & Enterprise College, Broughton

Mirror Me

Home.
I am myself.
My emotions are limitless,
Reaching the four corners of the world.

Then school comes,
I am an emotionless shell,
Trying to be free.
I'm all bottled up
And I can't be me.

At home, I am loud, weird and fun.
At school, I can't even crack out a pun.
At home, I'm not trapped in my own head.
At school, I'm so still I can be mistaken for dead.
I try to be myself.
I try to be free
But the only thing stopping it is Mirror Me.

Mirror Me tells me that I'm wrong
And it makes me a whole new person.
I forget my interests and pretend I'm not me,
I'm not free thanks to Mirror Me.

It's a game Mirror Me loves to play,
It's purely to cause me pain.
It steals my confidence which makes me scared

Because I'm not mentally prepared
For Mirror Me.

My home and school lives are polar opposites,
I'm always changing,
I can't be free,
I can't be free from
Mirror Me.

Katie G E Wilkinson (14)
Broughton Business & Enterprise College, Broughton

Notice

H appiness is overrated,
People cry, are sad, filled with emotion
And need help.
Notice the help they need,
The help I need.
It's the help, that secretly
We all want.
Notice that.

E nough of the fights in your head,
"Do it," they say, stop yourself.
Stop the constant pain, the suffering, the sorrow.
Notice that I am trying, trying to feel safe,
Feel safe alone with my thoughts.
Notice that.

L oneliness is the true killer,
Being suffocated by the lies you tell yourself.
"I'm fine." No, don't trust yourself,
Not now.
Notice that I have bled away my feelings,
No longer sad, it has bled away.
Notice that.

P lease notice,
Notice the scratches,
Notice the pain I am in, the pain I hide,

Notice the constant nagging of emptiness.
Cry, we want to cry.
The tears don't fall, nothing happens.
We are empty,
Notice because we are done, done with the pain.

Indiana Moore (13)
Broughton Business & Enterprise College, Broughton

This Is Me

I am not confident,
I am not popular,
I am not perfect,
I am me.

I grew up believing that I had no potential,
Starting in the shadows.
I grew up believing that I had no one to talk to,
All alone, the negative feelings inside me about to explode.
I grew up believing that I was a nobody,
Until I realised...

It's not about how you look or what you do,
It's not about what you wear and the latest fashion,
It's not about what you do at home and the way you live,
It's about what is in your heart and how you feel,
How you treat other people
And how you have an effect on them.

Some people need to realise that it's not about them,
Not about the newest trend,
Not about others' appearance,
Not about others' actions,
It's about others' feelings.

I am not black,
I am not white,

I am not brown,
I am a Muslim and I won't change for anyone!

Rabiyah Jamil (12)
Broughton Business & Enterprise College, Broughton

Trapped

All tied up in this hospital bed,
I can't get these words out of my head.
These demons echoing around the room,
The keepers come in and announce certain doom.

Lying on my bed waiting for the day I will one day break free
From all these demons that have forever cursed me
Or for the day where I will eventually
Have the strength to move
But perhaps that day will never come?

Yet, I seem to have missed
What could I have done to deserve this?
I am not a toy to be played with.
Trapped, staring at the ceiling
And at the floor,
Just wanting one thing,
To escape through that door.

To save myself from these wounds and scars
As I hear yet another beep
From the tubes, tests, needles and nurses
That pin me down while I sleep.
Parents, friends and family all weep
As I'm tied here on this hospital bed,
Those voices still in my head.

Casey Olive (13)
Broughton Business & Enterprise College, Broughton

Anti-Social Media

Click, click, click, whirr. Selfie, comment, like, share.
Don't point that thing at me!
I'm not just what you can see.
You can't see how I feel inside
Because I'm a girl who likes to hide
From lenses, glare, attention and light.
I don't want to appear on your feed
And feed your need for validation.
So don't include me in your fake lives
With your fake hair, fake tan and smile.
Filtering out reality.
Do you even know what is going on around you?
Can you tell your IRL from your social media hell?

500 likes aren't 500 friends, take a look around,
You'll be alone in the end.
Do you think about the fallout when you call out the lies?
Lies which turn into rumours
Spread like wildfire
Burning lives.

Anna Smyth (13)
Broughton Business & Enterprise College, Broughton

Glow

They can't see the past,
The tossing, turning nights.
They can't see the past,
The comments said from spite.

They don't see the fear,
The constant, nervous pain.
They don't see the fear,
The one that stays like a stain.

They can't feel the weight,
The one that keeps you down,
They can't feel the weight,
The one you feel all around.

But they will give you hope,
Make sure that you rise up.
But they will give you hope,
Will help you stand back up.

And they will show you light,
Remind you of tomorrow.
And they will show you light,
Help you through your sorrows.

You will make it through this,
You're stronger than you know.

You will make it through this,
They'll help you find your glow!

Megan Sloan (13)
Broughton Business & Enterprise College, Broughton

Labels

(Inspired by Prince EA)

Who would you be if the world never gave you a label?

I would be a shepherd, herding sheep down the right path.
I would be a comedian, making many laugh.
I would be black.
I would be white.
I would be Asian.
I would be a lone fisherman,
Catching fish with their bait.
I would be homeless, begging for my life.
I would be a father, watching my daughter become a wife.
I would be a police officer, putting all my life on the line.
I would be a royal, sipping on great wine.
I would be a cleaner, always brooming.
I would be a DJ, getting the crowd booming.
I would join the navy with my community of crewmen.

I would be all this because I'm the one, the only human.

Blake George Harrison (13)
Broughton Business & Enterprise College, Broughton

Escape Poetry

I grew up believing that magazine models were perfect,
That 'Instagram sensations' had never heard of Photoshop
And that they all had beautiful lives.

I grew up surrounded by faultlessness,
Stunning actresses swimming in money,
Falling in love with whoever they pleased;

Because they could.
They all had the power - somehow - to have
No flaws.

No weaknesses. All strengths.
No foulness, just grace;
And always perfect.

But then I realised,
I am not foul either.

I am not weak.
I am not vulnerable
And, most importantly, I am not perfect...

And that's a good thing -
Because no one is perfect.

Alisha Dahya (13)
Broughton Business & Enterprise College, Broughton

Hold On

Hold on, I still want you
Come back, I still need you.
Let me take your hand, I'll make it right.
I swear to love you all my life.

'Cause you've broken me
A million pieces around my feet.
You couldn't say to me it's going to be better.
And you took my heart, left behind a healing scar.
Medicine can only go so far
To help you get better, but you're still broken.

I never got the chance to say I love you,
Without you, there's nothing to do.
Leaving this world was one thing but saying goodbye is another.

I pulled you in to feel your heartbeat.
Could you hear me screaming, "Please don't leave me."

Hold on, I still need you...

Safa Beg (13)
Broughton Business & Enterprise College, Broughton

I Grew Up Believing

I grew up believing you are your label,
But these labels are not me, nor you,
They are just shells,
Ones we are forced to live in and to carry around every day.

This rhyme... 'Sticks and stones may break my bones
But words will never hurt me',
It doesn't work like that.
Every time I walk through these doors, I think to myself,
Please, no one comment on my appearance,
Please, no one make fun of what I'm wearing,
And then I think to myself, *why do I care?*
Why do I care about people's opinions?

I am not perfect,
I don't want to be perfect,
I just want to fit in,
I want to be me.

Eleanor McWilliams (13)
Broughton Business & Enterprise College, Broughton

I Think People Should Know

I think people should know
That my attitude really blows.
They think I am joking,
Aggression begins poking.
They think that I'm messing
Because they just keep pressing.

I'm now ticking out of time,
Trapped inside of my own mime.
Feel like I'm gonna blow,
All my loved ones do not know.
People took away my choice,
Left me here without a voice.

So now I can no longer speak,
Feeling like my life has peaked.
They think they know how it feels,
But they can't break through my peel.
No longer having any fun,
That's it, I think I am done.

Bobby Higham (13)
Broughton Business & Enterprise College, Broughton

Where You Need To Be

As a young child,
I always assumed that boys had to like blue
And girls had to like pink.
When my mum told me I was wrong,
I was ecstatic.
I was obsessed with blue.
The same thing happened when I was told I could like girls
But I'm not a girl anymore
And that probably came as more of a shock.

Some people have put up barriers.
"You're not a real boy until you have the surgery."
But if you want to be happy,
You do things in your own time.
Surround yourself with supportive people,
Eventually, you'll get to where you need to be.

Noah Campbell Beith (13)
Broughton Business & Enterprise College, Broughton

I Am Not...

I am not tall,
I am not confident,
I am not mean,
I am not sad,
I am not cool,
I am me!

I am not white,
I am not black,
I am not brown,
I am not green,
I am not purple,
I am me!

It doesn't matter what you look like,
It doesn't even matter who you are,
It is what's on the inside that counts,
Be your own kind of wonderful.
These are just labels,
Don't take them on board.
Set yourself free from your shell,
Uncover your true self.
It doesn't matter what people think,
Believe in yourself.

Lottie Carter (13)
Broughton Business & Enterprise College, Broughton

Feelings

I grew up believing that words can't hurt me,
Yet I realise how wrong I was.
We are taught to stand strong,
Ignoring the negative comments.

Some may brush it off,
Yet others are torn down by it,
Comment by comment, their image of themselves changes.

Then the questioning begins,
What if they are right?
As they question, they believe it more and more,
Feeling as if what people say is true.

They feel like talking to someone won't help
But it can.

I am not perfect,
Nor is anyone else
But I am me.

Beth Barker (13)
Broughton Business & Enterprise College, Broughton

A Cry For Help

To this day she hates the pressure of social media,
The need to get likes and followers,
The self-hate when she sees others picture perfect,
Popular and happy with their friends.

This doesn't help her anxiety,
The need to escape reality and fly away.
The pills aren't working and she's giving up on life
And the cuts and scars from self-harm want siblings.

She's losing control and can't stop.
Falling off a cliff into a pit of eternal darkness,
She can't escape or get out,
She begins to scream and shout.

Frances Grace Park (13)
Broughton Business & Enterprise College, Broughton

In The Shadows

I started in the shadows,
Days slowly went by,
I didn't tell anyone then
But now I wish I'd tried.

Persistent, never-ending pain,
These demons keep on pressing me,
Darkness and close to home flame,
I try and tell an adult, they say, "Grow up."
I disagree.

Bullying and hatred have become my every day,
All I want to do is hideaway,
I decided to go to my teacher,
He had that special feature.

He made it all go away,
I am happy every day,
I'm finally free,
I am full of glee.

Rory Hastings (13)
Broughton Business & Enterprise College, Broughton

Racism

To this day, I hate racism
The way people are judged for things they can't control.

How they are put through pain
For the onlookers' satisfaction and gain.

Why should they be judged by the colour of their skin
When they can't control the bodies they end up in?

To bystanders, it is a simple game
But to victims, it hurts more than words can explain.

Offensive remarks are thrown
Each word like a bullet to the head.

What makes you better than them?
This game needs to stop.

Amy Askam (13)
Broughton Business & Enterprise College, Broughton

Anxiety

Anxiety,
Feelings bottled up inside of you,
No one to talk to,
Struggling to cope,
Not wanting to go to school,
Not wanting to go out with friends
because you feel like you are the only one
who is going through this,
You feel like the whole world is against you,
You feel like you're not good enough for anyone,
Then things start to get better,
Like a weight has been lifted off your shoulders
because you have finally talked to someone
about your feelings

Libby Gibson (13)
Broughton Business & Enterprise College, Broughton

You Can't Control Me...

I'm not a doll you think you can control...
When I was a kid I believed we were really close,
That we told each other everything,
But now I'm not so sure,
It feels like all you do is push me around.

We all need to understand that in this world...
We are all something!

I'm tired of being pushed around;
This is my life and I have a right in this world.
We aren't here for nothing,
We are all brought into this world to be something!

Jenna Cross (13)
Broughton Business & Enterprise College, Broughton

Families

F ormula One means everything to me and my dad
A is for an awesome sister
M y family is everything to me,
    they take me on amazing adventures
I mpossible to forget
L oving, they help me all the time and I love them
I rritating but it is always in a funny way
E verything we do is exciting
S couts is what my mum started in the village,
    it is still going strong to this day.

Hayden Cooke (13)
Broughton Business & Enterprise College, Broughton

Influenced

When I was a kid, I used to dwell on people on social media
I'd wish my life was as perfect as theirs
I'd wish I looked the way they did
I'd wish I could have that many likes on my posts
I'd wish I was as happy as them
I'd wish I was exactly like them
But in reality, they aren't that perfect either
Everyone has their faults
And no kid should have to grow up
Believing they have to look or be like those on social media.

Emma Reynolds (13)
Broughton Business & Enterprise College, Broughton

Social Media

It's always there,
There is no escape,
People living their perfect lives,
Each mean comment like a knife,
It's there when you're at home,
It can leave you feeling alone.

You are not defined by your profile,
The things people say online are vile,
They will hide behind a screen,
Because they know what they're saying is mean,
Online lives are fake,
Happiness is something you shouldn't take.

Rebecca Wright (13)
Broughton Business & Enterprise College, Broughton

I Am Me

I am not black...
I am not white...
I am not blue...
I am not purple...
I am me.

Doesn't matter what your appearance is like,
It only matters what is in your soul.
Unless you have revealed who you are on the inside
No one can judge you.
They don't know the true you,
It's what your interior is like instead of your exterior,
Be individual,
Love yourself,
Be your own kind of beautiful.

Aaisha Patel (13)
Broughton Business & Enterprise College, Broughton

We Live Like This

I grew up believing life was a journey
Of happiness and fun
But my friend killed himself
And my dad had a gun.
We should love, not hate,
Play games and be comrades.
Is that too much to ask
Or does it always have to be like the past?
People are black and white, I don't care,
But for some reason, people get a scare.
No matter gay or straight
We should accept each other
And be mates.

Harry Harmer (13)
Broughton Business & Enterprise College, Broughton

Depression

Depression strikes hard
When you least expect
Because I always see these families
Getting destroyed and wrecked
It tears me apart
That people think life = death
People need to relax
And take a breath
Everyone has a future
That needs to be explored
All you need to do
Is open your bedroom door.

Isaac Jones (13)
Broughton Business & Enterprise College, Broughton

Beauty...

The definition of beauty begins with the word love.
Beauty doesn't always mean being pretty and handsome,
It means to be kind
And have a nice personality.
Even if you are pretty,
Even if you have the best figure
And have the worst personality
I wouldn't class you
As the definition of beauty.

Emily Saunders (14)
Broughton Business & Enterprise College, Broughton

Outer Space

When I lose my gravity
I can't escape
And I'm stuck in the dark
Of outer space
No one can hear my voice out here
All alone
But the silence is so loud
I plug my ears.

So I'll stay
All alone
In the dark of outer space
The silence of outer space.

Saira Latif (12)
Broughton Business & Enterprise College, Broughton

Grandpa

I can't describe the pain,
The mark you left,
The cruel choice of Satan
Took you away.
I remember the good
And the bad.
The evil puff of smoke
Took away the life you had
But till this day
Your beat goes on!
If I could turn back time...

Archie Macleod (13)
Broughton Business & Enterprise College, Broughton

Why Me?

Sticks and stones will break my bones,
Will hurt my feelings,
Will make me feel alone
But the worst thing is
It goes on and on
Every single day,
Just on and on.
Why just me?
What did I do?
How would you feel if I did this to you!

Rian Bowes (14)
Broughton Business & Enterprise College, Broughton

This Is Me!

Who am I?
What am I?
Where do I stand?
These are a few things I'm learning to understand.

I will not be judged.
I will not be changed.
This is me
And I like the way I am!

Khadijah Patel (13)
Broughton Business & Enterprise College, Broughton

Growing Old

Isn't it funny how time goes so fast?
As I sit here looking at the future,
I'm deliberating my past.

With memories of my youth,
Those days filled with sun,
Family times, not a care in the world,
Laughing in the sun.

The friends I have made
And the enemies too,
The games in the schoolyard,
The things we would do!

The days spent at work, grafting for a living,
The relentless chores, no boss ever forgiving
And then off to war to serve country and queen,
The memories I have, those images can't be unseen.

I have nurtured my children
And done them proud,
My wife, my best friend,
Last seen in her shroud.

They say life's a game we all have to play
And play it I have each and every day.

So now the time has come to say my goodbyes,
To embark on my journey up into the sky.

So please welcome me Lord into your land
As time has now left me,
Slipped through my fingers like grains of sand...

Heidi Elizabeth Walkden (13)
Oulder Hill Community School, Rochdale

Insecurities

Help, my looks are taking over my head,
Hardly waking up in the morning,
Drowning in my own tears,
Always walking into school like a clown.

Why can't I be like those girls?
I'm so alone, I can't make any friends,
They'll judge me.

My brain hurts, it's taking over all my feelings,
Why? Why do I have to feel like
I have to isolate myself from safety?
Terrified, depressed, loneliness, helpless,
I'm falling down the stairs, never getting to the top.
Lying at the bottom of the stairs, hopeless.

Always crying myself to sleep.
What's wrong with me?
I have insecurities, yes,
That's what is wrong with me.

Naomi Borg (12)
Oulder Hill Community School, Rochdale

Global Warming

Free the world of global warming
The cruelty and the waste
The sea of all the plastic
And all in good haste.

The animals in the Arctic
Are all losing their home
They're losing their food
And most of their biome.

Clear the sky of smoke
The pollution of the air
Alert people about what they're doing
As most are unaware.

Save the turtles of all the plastic
Buy a metal straw
The fish from eating microbeads
And dead animals drifting to shore.

Free the world of global warming
The cruelty and the waste
The sea from all the plastic
And all in good haste!

Matilda Glendinning (12)
Oulder Hill Community School, Rochdale

School

School, children hate it,
I don't understand why.

It is a place to learn new things
In an enjoyable way.

I know some lessons can be boring
But they should not just skip them.

Instead, they should endure and show resilience
Whilst waiting for an exciting lesson.

In that case, they will be rewarded by enduring
And enjoying lessons.

But for those who skip lessons
Their jobs and college choices will be compromised.

Just because they skipped a few English classes,
They can't get their dream job.

That is why you should never skip class.

Aziz Ahmad
Oulder Hill Community School, Rochdale

Equality

Gender is not a choice,
It's great, we all have a voice,
Let it go... man, woman, rich or poor,
We are born with much, much more.

Everyone should be in a world where there is peace
And not a world where you judge by only their face,
We all experience the same feelings,
After all, we are all human beings.

We all have ears that are able to listen
And we use them to hear other people's opinions.
Why shouldn't everyone be treated the same?
To have equal rights, that should be our aim.

Men and women all have their roles,
It's our target, to reach our goals.

Laibah Sohail (12)
Oulder Hill Community School, Rochdale

Life

You should live life to the fullest,
It is for your very best.

You should live life to the fullest,
Buy a house, build a nest.

You should live life to the fullest,
Have a family of your own.

You should live life to the fullest,
Become a scientist, build a clone.

You should live life to the fullest,
Go on holiday, have some fun.

You should live life to the fullest,
Go to the beach, bathe in the sun.

You should live life to the fullest
As you already know,
Because you never know when you'll die
Or how life's gonna go.

Igor Kadima
Oulder Hill Community School, Rochdale

Fake Real Friends

Friends are like angels
they keep bad away.
Most come and go
but the real ones are here to stay.

They use you and abuse you
through the shadow of my fears.
They don't care about you
even through your tears.

Cut fake friends out your life
before they backstab you with a knife.
Treat your friends with respect and loyalty,
don't treat them like royalty.

Your friends come first
even if they make you burst.
Friends are always there
even if you think they will go.
They are here to support you
everywhere you go.

Rebecca Andrew & Libby Mort (12)
Oulder Hill Community School, Rochdale

Racism

Racism comes in many forms,
Colour, shape, sizes and all.
It hurts my feelings deep inside,
With the disrespectful names you call.

Why can't we be treated as equal,
Instead of by our faith,
The world would be a better one,
Racism is a big disgrace.

I shouldn't have to be worried,
My religion is my choice,
My views are of my own,
I shouldn't hide my voice.

It makes me upset thinking,
Racism exists today,
In the multicultural world we live in,
This is not okay.

Zara Shaukat (13)
Oulder Hill Community School, Rochdale

Why Do I Feel This Way?

Why do I feel this way?
Why, why do I feel this way?
Lonely, depressed.

I have no one,
No one to laugh with,
No one to make a happy memory with.

My brain and my heart are fighting,
Is everything wrong or is nothing right?

My feelings take over my entire body,
If only you could see what is happening to me.

I'm lost in an ocean of despair and sadness,
Please, please can someone find me.

Aimee Louise Marland
Oulder Hill Community School, Rochdale

Believe In Us

I lie in the deep,
The shadows of the rest,
I just need some belief,
That would be the very best.

The nervousness destroys me,
From the inside out.
I'm just like a bee
Out and about - worrying about the rain.

Only a few believe me,
Only a few help,
We need help,
We're like a poor, poor fish stuck in kelp.

We are still human.

Joel David Crabtree (12)
Oulder Hill Community School, Rochdale

Sit By The Door

Sit by the door
And close your eyes,
Think of the breeze
That is calm and nice.

Sit by the door
And sing a song,
Clap out the beat
With your hands and feet.

Sit by the door
And read a book,
Think of the words
That lured you in.

Sit by the door,
Open your eyes,
Remember your loved ones
And your happy times.

Aneesa Mahroof (12)
Oulder Hill Community School, Rochdale

Cruelty

Lives ruined, hope is lost
Others crying just because
You said these things to their face
Confined inside, their joy erased.

Your hurtful words as sharp as spears,
Yet you carried on for years and years
Your look, your grin, your evil laugh,
That single word you can't take back.

They've asked you, "Stop!" They begged you, "Please!"
But you only gave them more and more needs
You gave them pain and broken bones
But only the ones who were on their own.

You think you're right but you're always wrong.
With every hateful word, parts have gone
You leave them afraid, you leave them depressed
Because you believe your actions are tests.

They say, 'Sticks and stones may break my bones',
But what is enough, a broken nose?
They always say karma's going to get you
You didn't believe them until it met you.

An arsenal of names fired at you
And you had no ideas on what to do.

You asked them for help, you begged them, "Please,"
It was then you realised that you had made enemies.

Liliana L Moore (12)
St Bede's High School, Blackburn

Regret...

I think I speak up for all of us
when I say that regret changes us.
It grasps you by the hand
and drowns you in a sea of sorrow;
it doesn't give you a break
neither today
nor tomorrow.
It tears down the confidence
that you have built...
and replaces it
with a tower of guilt.

It compels you
to question,
"What did I say?"
"What did I do?"
But then lets you fall flat
in a cave of humility
full of bats.

Bats that are screaming
and screeching
at you...
"Why did you do that?"

Through all of your fears
you fight back,

reach the tunnel
and head for the light.
You then realise that
regret is just an
illness
and you fight it back with
Forgiveness!

Enrikas Juselis (12)
St Bede's High School, Blackburn

Sometimes There Is No Bright Side

Sometimes I am unsure of my purpose,
Sometimes I am unsure of my worthiness,
Sometimes I feel made up,
Sometimes I can have an utter breakdown,
Sometimes I get mad for no reason.

My body, brain, eyes and ears see and hear,
All I can do is think,
My life is controlled, uncared for and unseen.
I feel the pain,
The pain for others and myself.
Thoughts of death convey through my mind.
The living atom I am will disintegrate into nothing.

The creation of me was sure a mistake,
It makes my heart ache.
If I had the choice of life and death,
Death would be portrayed upon me as it is my destiny.
I don't bring joy but irritation.

I have dreams but no faith,
I have nightmares but no confidence.
People are things I try to avoid,
The feelings just take over,

I have achievements,
I have family,
I have friends,
But I have no me.

Roan Schofield (13)
St Gabriel's RC High School, Bury

War On Racism

Again and again, we stand on the same path
And walk the same way.
They are the ones that want to make a game
That no one wants to play.
Never do we greet each other with a hello or hi,
We don't make the effort, not even a try.

The only words that come out are, "Terrorist, white, black."
Segregation carries on though it was stopped a while back.
We are one species, one human race,
Yet all that we care about is the colour of the face.

Hit, smack, blood, violence breaks out,
Words are the cause of this no doubt.
Every day, this war leaves us with scars,
But we are all people and none of us are from Mars.

People need to see the silver light,
But all there is is a racial fight,
If you take a minute to know the person beside you
And don't have a closed mind,
Then maybe you will be surprised with what you find.

Maimoona Latif (13)
St Gabriel's RC High School, Bury

Inside

When people look at you and they judge you
'Cause of the mistakes that you made in the past,
People have been spreading about you, that's untrue,
Out of a thousand, I feel an outcast.
Trying to keep a smile on my face every day,
Inside, my heart's a scrunched up piece of paper,
I keep choking on every word that I say,
Regretting keeping silent sooner or later.

Anti-depressants aren't working, they're useless,
They taste disgusting, it's even ridiculous.
Who knew it was this hard to fit in
And this world that we're living in, is trippin'.

No one will understand, they'll think I'm crazy,
Nothing inside of me, just emptiness,
Can't find anything that rhymes with crazy,
When I try to talk I find myself speechless.

It's like being in a box and there's no way out,
No one's gonna hear you, even if you shout.
I wish it could go like a switch,
The same way people tell on you and you call them a snitch.
Your heart shatters into a million pieces,
When people look at you like you're faeces.

Isaora Tandy Shima (12)
St Peter's RC High School, Manchester

Labels, Colours And All That Stuff

Days when you can hardly lift your head,
The pain, too much for even yourself.
That tiresome sensation eating away at you,
Seconds like minutes, minutes like hours, hours like days,
Hands wrapped tightly around you,
Your only source of comfort.
Take a second to remember what Martin Luther King did,
Could you ever do that?
Stand up for people used as slaves
Because of their skin?
No.
But instead, you deal with people calling you,
'Black' or 'white' or 'Asian',
'Chinese', 'Mongolian' or 'Malaysian'.
Even that alone is not enough
But not applying for a job because of your 'background'?
You hate yourself, thinking, *why can't I be... them?*
All because of...
Labels, colours and all that stuff.

Head throbbing,
Feeling shameful just to step out of your front door,
Thoughts, looks and questions,
Enough to keep you hidden in your cloud of despair,
The fluid that everyone calls water,
Salty and bitter,

Rolling down your cheek with the sense in your mind
That no one cares!
Curled up like a snail in your only hideout, your home
Because people can't help but discriminate you for you.
Take a second to remember what Rosa Parks did.
Could you ever do that?
Sit down on a bus and stand up for where you sit?
No.
You get pushed and tossed and kicked around like a football
All because of...
Labels, colours and all that stuff.

Feeling left out,
Excluded,
Not part of,
The hall goes quiet when you arrive,
So quiet you can hear a pin drop.
The second you leave, everyone laughs and points at you.
You sit at the back to avoid
The 'hilarious jokes' made at you.
Anger and hurt all in one
But you can see past that
And then you realise,
You have been hiding away your inner beauty and courage,
All because of...
Labels, colours and all that stuff.

Glory Odubanjo
St Peter's RC High School, Manchester

Why Am I Not Good Enough?

Why is it that when you arrive at school
Roaring lions await you
Ready to pick apart every single insecurity that appears?
Isn't it unfair
That people stare
And cackle at you?
Why am I not good enough?

We come to school every day
To be prepared for our future.
But, what type of future are we being prepared for?
One full of peer pressure;
One full of lies;
One full of rumours ruining people's lives.
I ask why am I not good enough?

Education is what school is for, yet,
What are we being educated on?
How to deal with criticism;
How to deal with depression;
How to deal with all your memories turned sour.
Not because of you,
Because of self-centred, egotistical people that ruin days;
No weeks;
Years of people's lives.
I want to know why am I not good enough?

'They say sticks and stones
May break my bones but words will never hurt me'.
What about all the children
That run home crying because of
A single cruel thing they have heard
Someone say about them?
Together we all ask, why are we not good enough?

The truth is you are good enough,
Nothing anyone ever says or does can change that.
No amount of hatred or violence can change that.
Your flaws are what make you different from everyone else.
Together we chant, "We are good enough!"
Nothing anyone says or does will change that.
You are strong!
You are powerful!
You are unique!
And that is what matters.
Not any lies that come out of someone's mouth.
We are all good enough.

Alexa Murkste
St Peter's RC High School, Manchester

It Kills Me!

The one word that scares me, bullying,
Verbal, physical or cyber, it still scares me to this day.
The nasty comments on social media,
The painful bruises on my body,
The words,
They hurt me the most.
It kills me!

It is like they flew out of the bully's mouth
And raced to enter inside of me.
Slowly, it broke me up piece by piece,
Eventually, it affected my health.
I was diagnosed with depression,
Thousands of other victims
Recognised with anxiety, mental health and more.
Slowly, time went by.
Fifteen years later, I haven't changed,
Yes, them same upsetting words
Whirling inside of me to this day.
Do you want to know why?
Just because of one thing,
Bullying,
It kills me!

Yes, bullying,
The situation that people think is a minor issue,
The young people killing themselves just because of bullying.

I'll tell you what the worst part is,
The bully moves on as that was a small chapter of their life,
Which I guess they have forgotten.

I hate it!
I absolutely hate it!
It irritates me
That this horrifying behaviour on teens,
Children or even adults can sometimes destroy your life.
It kills me!
It kills me!
It really kills me!

Kieran Asif
St Peter's RC High School, Manchester

Planting The Seed

In a beautiful garden, she plants a seed
Which eventually grows into a tree.
The tree eventually grows a branch
And the branch eventually grows apples that you catch.

The beautiful garden is no longer seen,
It locks the gates like it has never been.
Vibrant colours turn black and white
As it slowly loses its bright light.

The beautiful garden had stabs it received
From growing roots that started from a seed.
The only cure is to cut the tree down,
However, the gates are locked with a frown.

The wicked witch that planted the seed,
Is the only one with access to the key.

In another beautiful garden, she plants a seed
Which eventually grows into a tree.
The tree eventually grows a branch
And the branch eventually grows apples that you catch.

She decides which tree she plants in your mind,
Anxiety, depression and a barrier to hide behind.
What if she decided to be free
And grow a healthy tree?

Alicja Baczkowicz (13)
St Peter's RC High School, Manchester

Today In Our Society

Today in our society,
We are judged on the colour of our skin,
The race we have been given,
But why, why should we be judged,
Compared, when we are equally all the same?
Black is beautiful, white is beautiful
And the history is there to prove these facts,
But still hating people continue to stab us in our backs.

Today in our society,
Children are getting bullied because of their skin tone,
But why, why are they being criticised
By such heartless people?
They don't have a problem so why do others?
All these loving children pray for justice someday,
But will they get the chance to live their lives the same way?

Today in our society,
People rage, raging about if the world will ever change,
The hating people will never stop,
But these hating people should be shut up.
These harsh words could affect someone's life,
So ask yourself
Were your cruel words worth the loss
Of someone else's life?

Arianna Voniece Arielle Allen (13)
St Peter's RC High School, Manchester

You Are You

Now I know, people can be rude or cruel,
But now I know that lots of people are racist.

So people think you're a bad person because you're black or white,
Where people think you're fire and they're water,
But just stop, you are you and no one can change that.

So you are you and we can stop racism by respecting other skin tones.
Now listen, I may feel anxious if someone's being cruel to us
But what are we doing being cruel to others?

Now that people think we'll die and they'll lie
But this is wrong for what colour we are,
Because you are you and no one can stop you from being yourself.

People, we can be quick to stop this
Because if we slow down we might never be able to stop this,
So it's now or never to end this.

And then we will rise and the cruel will fall hopefully forever,
Because you are you.

Blake Joyce
St Peter's RC High School, Manchester

The Lost Ones

Socks, shoes, books
Are things we've all lost.
Aren't these valuable to you?

We're tired of your games,
Every day a life is lost to you.
It's like you love the fame
And the pain that we feel.
You've taken people we love,
It was a terrible cost.

We're tired of your games,
We hate you and the tricks that you play.
Young children are gone because of your evilness.
We're finally breaking the chains of suicide.
You're no longer welcome here,
So leave us in peace.

We're tired of your games,
Don't you dare come back.
The battles are over,
No one will ever be swallowed by your agonising pain.
Children, teenagers and adults
Will never kill themselves again.
If we all stand as one,
Valuable people will never be lost to suicide again.

Jennifer Adesanya (13)
St Peter's RC High School, Manchester

Triggered

They say that it only takes a few seconds to pick up a gun,
But when you've never done it before...
It can be much harder than you think
To end someone's life that quick.

How would you feel?
Standing there, still.
Gun in hand,
Trigger ready.
Someone's else's fate:
In your hands.

He could've had kids.
He could've had a wife.
He could've made something of himself.
Then...
Bang!

Gone,
It's all gone.
What did you do?

Ashamed.
You looked to the ground
That's when you saw it.
His future.
Drip, drip, dripping away
Along with his blood.

That's when you knew
You had robbed him:
Of his possessions,
Of his future,
Of his life,
Everything...

Jessica Belle Stockley (13)
St Peter's RC High School, Manchester

Colour Doesn't Matter

Colour doesn't matter
Let's make this world better.
Judging on the imagination you don't know
Makes the situation worse
Don't be the attacker
Don't be the hater because you always matter.

Some people carry their honour in a flag
And of their nationality, they brag
They feel superior and they differentiate
And against those who are different they discriminate.

So many people are still judged by their race,
For these people who judge by race
There should never be a place.

What matters is what lies within,
We live in this so-called democracy
Where we can never be free,
Use your imagination wisely,
Tour the world,
Laugh,
Grow strong
For colour doesn't matter,
What does matter is what lies within.

Khadija Irfan (13)
St Peter's RC High School, Manchester

It's A Violation Thing

Let's talk about racism,
About inequalities,
About crime.
I've been holding in how I feel
And I think that this is the time.
They think that it's okay.
These white people aren't fine,
Let's talk about slavery,
Let's talk about whips.
We work all day,
Our sweat, the way it drips.

Glock...
The only word they know,
Is the one that makes us triggered,
They calmly pull the trigger,
I remember how I quivered.

I see something...
I watch our family die
But we're hiding in the closet,
My face is too dry to cry,
My parents' lives were just deposits.
Their experience of racism,
The pain they can't feel,
The bullet between their eyes,
Dear white people, feelings are real.

David Abioye (12)
St Peter's RC High School, Manchester

Doomsday

Wouldn't you imagine
Of a heavenly Earth
Free of imperfections
Just as God planned?

You would, would you not?
Sadly, this doesn't seem to be the case.

At least not for us, anyway.
You see, there is something
Called climate change
That can't make this dream possible again.

Climate change, sounds sad, doesn't it?
For me and you, there's no stopping it.

Burning fossil fuels
Is as easy as counting from one to three.
Maybe we could prevent it...
Destroying all these trees.

Wasting these resources,
Selfishness strikes once again,
No one thinks about anyone else,
The unfortunate living in vain.

So please, just hear me out
So we can stop climate change without a doubt.

Osasumwen Aimuyo (12)
St Peter's RC High School, Manchester

One More Day

Fizzle, it was a hot sunny day,
Everyone was having fun, underneath the sun.
Thunder, all of a sudden, it started to rain,
People wondered why it had changed.
Lightning struck heavier than ever before,
What had changed?

Storms occurred all over the world,
The sun was gone, there was no shine.
There was no perfect blue sky,
Just clouds, just fog,
No birds, they all fell down to the ground.

People fled, ran for their lives but it was too late,
The news said 'Global warming's twelve years is up',
But he lied because this is because of us!

We doomed the world with pollution and death,
All it took was one hot day.
Don't make tomorrow be our last one,
Because there will be no more us!

Rianna Holden (12)
St Peter's RC High School, Manchester

Two Thousand And Nineteen

It still agonises me
How in two thousand and nineteen
Sexism is still a thing against women,
Do men think they're better than us?

It still exasperates me
How sexism is still worshipped and praised,
Do men think they're stronger than us?

It still disheartens me
How sexism is still used as a tool,
Do men think they're smarter than us?

Don't allow yourself to be swallowed
By the sexism sweeping this nation.
But yet an everyday act of sexism,
Twists, tangles and distorts our world
Like a moth to a flame.
Let's break down these barriers
Of hatred and discrimination.

This needs to stop here and now,
In two thousand and nineteen.

Keziah Kazadi (13)
St Peter's RC High School, Manchester

A Knife To The Skin

This poem is about knife crime,
The question, does it need to rhyme?
Sadly we couldn't stop it in time,
Knife crime is sour like lime.

Knife crime, it's sharp,
Never going to match the melody of a harp,
Maybe it's jealousy,
Stabbing victims ambitiously.

People kill others because of the past,
Quickly five months, 100 victims couldn't last.
Lucky many come home with a cast,
Nervous people try to survive by running fast.

Keeping people hostile,
Always running that extra mile,
Having many knives in a pile,
Shredding their own file.

Sharper than a shark's tooth,
You never feel safe under a roof,
You can hear its howl.

Yahya Hussein (11)
St Peter's RC High School, Manchester

Monster That's Lurking

Mother knows best,
She always says
I am as precious as gold.
It breaks my heart to see her disowned.

She tucks me in bed
And walks downstairs
To a drunken monster
Who doesn't care.

Bruises are left,
Scars are shown,
The only plaster she has
Is the make-up she owns.

She works long shifts
And walks in the freezing cold.
Scared to come home to the evil monster
That can break her bones.

That so-called monster
Was once the perfect dad
And husband.

He soon suffered from depression,
From the long hours he was working,
He soon turned to alcohol
And he is now known as the monster that's lurking.

Thandi Sibanda
St Peter's RC High School, Manchester

Breakdown

Breakdown,
That's what it is,
Climate and ecological breakdown,
That's what we have found.

It's a hoax they say,
Global warming, how could they?
Plastic, pollution,
Destroying the world for us all.

Eleven years,
Not for me but for us all,
Yet you're skipping around,
Like it's a ball.

Focus on your education,
That's what they say,
How could we
When there's no future anyway.

Worrying about the Earth,
The Earth that is our home,
You destroyed it,
The Earth we have evolved.

I know we're not all the same,
But we're all humans,
Enough to change the game.

Aliyah Soyinka (13)
St Peter's RC High School, Manchester

The Blanket Of Doom

Thoughts circling,
What should we do?
The world is spinning,
Is all of this true?

The blanket of doom drapes upon us,
Horses whine, bees buzz.
Global warming, like a shadow it hovers,
Families will die, even your mothers.

Thoughts circling,
What should we do?
The world is spinning,
Is all of this true?

Sea levels rising, ice is melting,
Dead bodies lie around, it's very revolting.
The world will end,
It won't ever mend.

Thoughts circling,
What should we do?
The world is spinning,
Is all of this true?

But this can stop, only if we make it,
Recycle things, reuse and recycle it!

Alisha Akram (12)
St Peter's RC High School, Manchester

Climate Change

A feeling to be scared,
The end may be near,
If there is no change,
Humanity will be wiped out.

Change in the environment,
The polluted air,
Affecting our bodies,
Animals die,
As the world gets hotter and hotter,
With every particle of carbon dioxide,
Filling the air,
Global warming is also near.

Sea levels rising,
The cause of this,
Glaciers and mountains of ice,
Melting and breaking off into the sea.

Polar bears and penguins have nowhere to live,
As their homes are getting smaller.

To help stop this,
Reuse, recycle and reduce,
All the waste we use
And put in the landfill.

Nur-Aein Saidil (12)
St Peter's RC High School, Manchester

Bullying

Confused why I'm seeing this,
Confused why this is happening,
Confused why a person could even do this.
Bullying, the thing that can drag you down,
Rip you apart and make you feel like nothing.
Hurtful words crush your chest,
Making you feel like you've got nowhere to go
And no one to tell.
Crying in the night and feeling stranded
With that silly nickname made up by the bully.
Walking through the halls, names are being whispered
As the tears fall down the face of the little victim.
The most horrible thing that could happen to a person,
Scared about what's going to happen next.
Tell someone, make sure you tell someone.

Emma Louise Hennessy (14)
St Peter's RC High School, Manchester

Bullying

Words can mean a lot
But also make people sad,
Even when most of the time
You think you've done nothing bad.

Sometimes the words that hurt one the most
Come from friends.
It could be hilarious,
It could be depressing,
It all depends.

Words can hurt
And take your emotion all over the place,
Depression, anxiety, loneliness,
It's a very bad case.

These words make me feel
Like a fork in a bunch of spoons,
A big mistake,
I just want to be gone and break.

Words can mean a lot
But also make people sad,
Even when most of the time
You think you've done nothing bad.

Modupe Olowu (13)
St Peter's RC High School, Manchester

Think About It?

Death! It's like a sunken well
Where happiness, love and family
Are sucked like a black hole.
People yank their lives 'cause their hearts
Are trapped like a cell.
Those who are missed are never withered away
As their presence is marked like a mole.

Family problems, bullying, cyberbullying,
Hearing those excruciating words,
Doesn't it make your heart sink?
I have blinked away the tears.
Start thinking. Just think.
Think about grasping the hands
Of those who are willing to let go of life.

Bring them back to humanity as our lives matter.
We need our hearts.
Wow, death is really like a sunken well.

Gloria Kayenge (11)
St Peter's RC High School, Manchester

The Differences

Their words hurt like knives.
Their words tie you down
Like the Devil himself keeps you to torture you.

They say you're different, a monster, a freak,
A waste of space, a waste of oxygen,
But I tell you, don't let them pull the wool over your eyes,
They are the sheep who do not want to be themselves.
They follow the shepherd in the endless crowds,
But you have a gift that makes you yourself,
Not a sheep but a shepherd.

They say you're a monster,
They look for anything different about you,
But I say fantasise how you got it right
Now you're an author
Who leads the next generation with words.

Neo Cassidy (13)
St Peter's RC High School, Manchester

Stop Racism

R acism makes me upset because of how evil people are.
"**A** re we all one family?" Yes, we are
because we are equal and one family.
"**C** an we stop racism?" We can stop racism
by loving one another and respecting each other.
I am not racist because we cannot judge people for who
they are, we have different responsibilities.
S ign of peace is a key to stop racism because
it will make this world so much better.
M agnificent people live in this world so why can't everyone
show their wonderful talents? Then this world will be
amazing!

Danny Bradley (12)
St Peter's RC High School, Manchester

Sweets In A Bowl

Sweets in a bowl crashing down,
Red ones called names, blue called exclusion
And purple called bullying.

Bullying lurks around the corner,
Ready to catch its prey.
Every time you call someone a name,
A red sweet drops in slow today.

Calling someone ugly and leaving them out the group,
Causes a blue sweet to hover and then drop.

Once the mixtures have finished mixing purple pops
And the bowl starts overflowing until it drops.

Once on the floor society takes them away,
Then the sweets are spoilt so death awaits.

The glass bowl shatters
And the broken heart fades today...

Jane Rosana (12)
St Peter's RC High School, Manchester

A Broken Voice

A certain heartbeat flickers as it tries to convey,
A message to reveal that it is not okay.
This burning sensation that eats it inside,
Waves clash deep down; the pressure abides.

Silencing a heartbeat that tries to speak out,
Distress; anxiety this is what it's all about.
Wretched, untamed tongue which will never obey,
A rude spoilt soul - that is all they can say.

A destiny too strong to try and twist and turn,
A throat too stiff to try and speak and learn.
A certain heartbeat flickers as it tries to convey,
A message to reveal that is is not okay.

And it is truly not okay.

Izodosa Divina Osarenmwinda (13)
St Peter's RC High School, Manchester

Dangerous Destruction

Confusing thoughts racing through my mind,
We need a solution that we can find.
In just three seconds we ruined our world's beauty.
In just three seconds we ruined its purity.

Waves of plastic torture the whales,
Massive monster machines destroying the homes of the innocent.
We are so malevolent.

We need to work together.
We need some achievement.
We need some positivity.

We could recycle more
To save our world even more.
We could alter our ways
So we can make it to the fourth second.

'The time is always right to do what is right'.

Ashiq Ali Mirza (11)
St Peter's RC High School, Manchester

The Last Goodbye

As she stands on the roof
She looks down
At the world that was supposed to be nice,
At her friends who don't give a damn,
Tears stream down her face.

She looks up,
Taking her last breath,
Taking her last step,
She looks at her letter,
Tears fall down,
Leaving marks,
Goodbye.

She throws the letter down,
Counts to three
And jumps,
As she falls down
She screams, "Goodbye, bye."

The message is,
Care about people,
'Cause one day it might be too late
To say sorry,
To have respect,
To be nice.

Wiktoria Januszewska (13)
St Peter's RC High School, Manchester

Another Day

Another day in school
Getting beaten to the ground
I wish I wasn't alive
Everything is such a beehive.

Another day in school
I'm just one of the fools
Who get slapped, punched and kicked
And always getting picked.

It's all on repeat
A cycle of getting beat
Sometimes I question myself
And always wonder about my health.

Every single day, thoughts fill my head
As my friend once said,
"I'll be by your side."
But all of that was just lies.

Is it easier to just let go
Or should I just go with the flow?

Melissa Nguyen-Le (13)
St Peter's RC High School, Manchester

The Wise One

Education is the soil in the ground,
The knowledge that carries you around,
The amazing feeling of success,
The wonderful knowledge that makes you the best.
However, if penniless you will fall to the ground,
In poor countries, you will never be found.
Desperate for knowledge,
Desperate for glory,
Wanting a chance,
Wanting to change the world with fame,
Not wasting my life with video games,
Discovering secrets,
Curing diseases like gastroenteritis.
Unfortunate children that miss out on the fun,
Losing education,
Not being the wise lucky one.

Joshua Lo (12)
St Peter's RC High School, Manchester

Are We Really Equal?

You say we're equal when you give us weird looks!
You say we're equal when you still walk away from us!
You say we're equal when you don't want to be close to us!
Are we really equal?
Are we really equal when you curse at us?
Are we really equal when you tell us
To go back from where we came?
Are we really equal when you have expectations from us?
How do you think we feel?
How do you think we feel when you do all that?
We feel different.
You make us think that we are an outcast.
Equality is when we love, respect and care for each other.

Flourish Ugiagbe
St Peter's RC High School, Manchester

Racism, Racism, What Do You See?

Racism, racism what do you see?
Black, white, all from the same society.
People need to know
Our skin colours are not just for show.

So we say to them,
"What do you see?
Aren't I just like you
Or am I another wannabe?"

Another racist comment
That's all I ever hear
Bellowed down my ear.

Black is no different to white,
White is no different to black,
We are all the same,
In one big pack.

Racism, racism, what do you see?
Another problem in the world,
That means everything to me.

Cheloliseh Joseph Umeh (12)
St Peter's RC High School, Manchester

The Hidden Crime

Tears falling, hearts breaking,
A mother crying for her son,
Why? 'Cause someone thought he had a gun.

The innocent are losing,
The corrupt are winning,
How are we supposed to trust,
Trust you to serve and protect
When all we want is you to care?

White vs black, black vs white,
Who cares? You just wasted another life.
The street runs red
With blood and tears because of the police.

So here's my question,
How's this fair?
It's a crime that goes unpunished,
It's a murder that's unspoken.

Roda Afeworki (13)
St Peter's RC High School, Manchester

Bullying, Is It Bad?

Bullying, is it bad?
Yes, it is.
We have to show bullies that bullying is bad
Because it makes people very sad.
Some people even cry
And then they think to themselves,
I want to fly.
Fly to somewhere else,
Fly to where I am safe from bullies.
And the friends of the people are sad,
It made them mad.
"We've lost our friend," they said on the bench,
"And I think it's because of bullies.
How can we stop it,
Stop it for just a bit?"

We can stop it with teamwork.

Dominion Ugiagbe (12)
St Peter's RC High School, Manchester

The Unlucky Ones

Mental health is a raging beast
Murdering our innocent, young kids.
Depression, bullying, suicide, self-harm
Are what our kids are having
And their bullies are there, laughing.
Why aren't the kids telling anyone?
Sooner or later, they're gone,
Then their parents are feeling pain.
Inside, they're going insane.
I think kids shouldn't go through this,
All they want is a kiss.
Is this what kids want?
To look back and still be haunted?
So please, kids, just tell anyone you trust,
You are important.

Gamiel Bughaili (12)
St Peter's RC High School, Manchester

Social Media

Whatever goes up must go down,
Followers from Instagram soon all around,
Don't forget people are cruel,
So don't you dare act like a fool.

Because what you put on the Internet
Will never go down as people can see from all around.

They can expose you, expose your nudes
And everything else, you will only lose.

It can ruin you, it will hurt you.

It will start out as a meme,
Then a video,
You will go viral,
Then everyone will remember you
And the way your life spiralled.

Jakai Ucal McGlacken-Bryan (11)
St Peter's RC High School, Manchester

Confusing Thoughts

Confusing thoughts are racing through my mind,
I wake up in the morning and wonder why.
Why do I have to walk out of my house
And be judged only by the colour of my skin?
Not even made a sin.

I walk the streets concerned if I'm going to get beaten today
Or if it's finally going to be another way.
Always aware of my surroundings,
If I'm not, I'd be drowning.
Drowning in the tears of the thought
I have to worry for my life every day
Because of the colour of my melanin browning.

Shadeh Stone
St Peter's RC High School, Manchester

The Lost Ones

Some people we lost
Were involved with a knife.
We need to stop this,
Otherwise, more people will lose their life.

Some people die,
Some stay alive.
We need to stop this
Because to this day, more people carry knives.

Innocents or criminals
That doesn't matter.
We need to stop this,
Someone will die sooner or later.

This happens to us,
This happens to our family.
We need to stop this
Because people lose their lives rapidly.

Fabian Truszkowski (12)
St Peter's RC High School, Manchester

It's Not Our Fault

It's not our fault
and you can tell me that
our society is horrible,
that depression and bullying are a thing,
that people are dying at the hands of humans,
you can tell me,
that racism is not a problem,
that sexism is okay,
that humans are not destroying this Earth.
You can't tell me
that this society is not perfect
and it's our fault.

Now, read it in reverse order to see what life is really like.

Angel Taofeeqah Jimoh (13)
St Peter's RC High School, Manchester

Bullying

Bullying, bullying causes depression,
Myriads of children get insulted by their looks every day!

Then depression opens a ghastly, malicious gateway,
Causing damage to their souls.
Suicide, anxiety and deaths all start
From a simple malicious word,
Bullying.

One child may feel depressed by bullying,
The word roaring in their heads, in their minds,
The eerie, appalling word, bullying,
Can kill caring, innocent people.

Beauty Somoye (11)
St Peter's RC High School, Manchester

Racism

Confusing thoughts are racing through my mind,
I can't go to an airport without getting searched
And whenever I'm driving on the road,
I get pulled over for no reason.
Also, when I buy something from the store,
I get kicked out because
They think I'm going to steal something.

They always think we're carrying drugs,
They also assume that we have weapons,
When there's a crime being committed, they blame us.

Daniel Yemane Fesseha
St Peter's RC High School, Manchester

The Dangerous War

Help, the war is going to happen,
Lots of soldiers died.
People are evacuating to the UK,
Myriads of people and children died
And some are trapped.
The children are crying and hungry,
People are killed by bombs and pollution,
People are living in the debris.
I want to stop the war
And make all the countries that are in the war friendly
And help border partners.
I want the children to be safe
And not to be dead.

Dipto Obyadur (12)
St Peter's RC High School, Manchester

Existing

Since time began, Earth was one in a million.
The only planet which could support life that we know of.
The human race has only walked on the very ground of
Earth for over eight million years.
We are still a new species but now that we have discovered
fire-throwing rocks to kill bigger creatures,
Spikes and shields from fishing to power
When many really started to exist in this world.
But we still try to look for new places to call home.

Kai Douglas (12)
St Peter's RC High School, Manchester

Battling My Depression

I watched as the devious monster
Planned their next attack on me,
I'm covered in scars and marks,
Unpleasant I know.
I just can't help it when they take over my body,
It can be extremely vile.

It's like there's constantly a wrench around my throat
And they're not stopping the turning,
They are strangling me from the inside,
I can't do anything about it.
Help stop depression.

Fatou Mbye (13)
St Peter's RC High School, Manchester

Anxiety

Tear me to bits, that's how you thrive,
Watching me claw at my inside,
You're my master and I'm your slave,
More possessions of your own intentions
To mould and shape as you see fit.
You destroy a life so yours can grow.
I'm your masterpiece, why would you leave
When you can haunt me and alter my thoughts?

I hear you giggle in my dreams,
Behind the curtain you can't be seen.

Hamza Waseem (13)
St Peter's RC High School, Manchester

Bullying

Your heart breaks when you see the news
And an innocent child's photo is under the headlines,
'Bullied to death' or 'hung to death'.
Bullying is a virus that spreads around to hurt people...
Suicide is a disease that can never be cured.
This world is a cruel, bitter place.
Mothers and fathers are losing their children every single day.
We need to stop this beast called bullying!

Chanel Nicole May (12)
St Peter's RC High School, Manchester

It All Starts With A Knife

Knife crime is all you see here and there, everywhere.
People's lives are fading away,
I have nightmares about it every day.
Taking a knife along the streets,
Killing anyone they meet.
Bodies are spread on the floor,
I wish there were no knife crimes to explore.
Don't take people's lives
With your very pointy, dangerous knife,
Instead, get some help and clean yourself.

Divine Omose Omoijade (12)
St Peter's RC High School, Manchester

Suicide: A Force To Be Reckoned With

Suicide is an effect, it goes all around us,
Hunting down everyone in its path,
It peels and tears through any soul or body,
It has the power to do what it likes.
It has shaken us all with its power.
Suicide is a force to be reckoned with,
A power to ruin us all on the inside,
So we must come together to stop this illness
Before it hits us seriously
And we are done for good.

Aaron Tebu (12)
St Peter's RC High School, Manchester

Alone

Confusing thoughts are racing through my mind,
I feel alone, sad and scared.
People calling me names, stupid, dumb, lame,
I feel scared and isolated,
Lonely and abandoned.
Beaten up, called names,
Words all around my brain.
Rude text messages, nasty calls
And names called through the halls.

Josephine Ashiru (13)
St Peter's RC High School, Manchester

A World Unknown

Welcome to a world unknown,
Welcome to the wonder zone.
Welcome to Imagination Plaza,
Welcome to a world where you're the master.

Where dreams are as real as you and me
And fantasies are reality.
Where dragons soar high in the sky
And pencils taste like apple pie.

It's a world full of dreams,
A world where nothing's quite as it seems,
It's a world of unknown,
That you can call your own.

It's an escape
From the hate
And lies and deceit,
It's a world you could never beat.

It's a world where you're the creator,
Nothing else could be greater.
But sadly, it's only true
In dreams through and through.

We're so very sad you're gone,
This world was meant for everyone.
It's not something for you alone
For this is everyone's world unknown.

Jessica Waite (13)
Walton-le-Dale High School, Bamber Bridge

YOUNG WRITERS INFORMATION

We hope you have enjoyed reading this book – and that you will continue to in the coming years.

If you're a young writer who enjoys reading and creative writing, or the parent of an enthusiastic poet or story writer, do visit our website www.youngwriters.co.uk. Here you will find free competitions, workshops and games, as well as recommended reads, a poetry glossary and our blog. There's lots to keep budding writers motivated to write!

If you would like to order further copies of this book, or any of our other titles, then please give us a call or visit www.youngwriters.co.uk.

Young Writers
Remus House
Coltsfoot Drive
Peterborough
PE2 9BF
(01733) 890066
info@youngwriters.co.uk

Join in the conversation!
Tips, news, giveaways and much more!

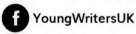 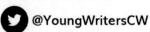